WEST SIDE

Based on a conception of Jerome Robbins

Book by
Arthur Laurents

Music by
Leonard Bernstein®

Lyrics by
Stephen Sondheim

Entire Original Production
Directed and Choreographed by
Jerome Robbins

ISBN 978-1-4234-5826-5

LEONARD
BERNSTEIN
Music Publishing
Company LLC

BOOSEY & HAWKES

AN IMAGEM COMPANY

DISTRIBUTED BY

HAL•LEONARD®
CORPORATION
7777 W. BLUEMOUND RD. P.O. BOX 13819 MILWAUKEE, WI 53213

For all works contained herein:
Unauthorized copying, arranging, adapting, recording, Internet posting, public performance,
or other distribution of the printed or recorded music in this publication is an infringement of copyright.
Infringers are liable under the law.

Visit Hal Leonard Online at
www.halleonard.com

How To Use The CD Accompaniment:
A melody cue appears on the right channel only. If your CD player has a balance adjustment, you can adjust the volume of the melody by turning down the right channel.

The CD is playable on any CD player, and is also enhanced so PC and MAC users can adjust the recording to any tempo without changing the pitch.

◆ AMERICA

TENOR SAX

Lyrics by STEPHEN SONDHEIM
Music by LEONARD BERNSTEIN

Copyright © 1957 by Amberson Holdings LLC and Stephen Sondheim
Copyright Renewed
This arrangement Copyright © 2011 by Amberson Holdings LLC and Stephen Sondheim
Leonard Bernstein Music Publishing Company LLC, Publisher
Boosey & Hawkes, Inc., Sole Agent
Copyright For All Countries   All Rights Reserved

4

◆ COOL

TENOR SAX

Lyrics by STEPHEN SONDHEIM
Music by LEONARD BERNSTEIN

Copyright © 1957 by Amberson Holdings LLC and Stephen Sondheim
Copyright Renewed
This arrangement Copyright © 2011 by Amberson Holdings LLC and Stephen Sondheim
Leonard Bernstein Music Publishing Company LLC, Publisher
Boosey & Hawkes, Inc., Sole Agent
Copyright For All Countries   All Rights Reserved

❸ I FEEL PRETTY

TENOR SAX

Lyrics by STEPHEN SONDHEIM
Music by LEONARD BERNSTEIN

Copyright © 1957 by Amberson Holdings LLC and Stephen Sondheim
Copyright Renewed
This arrangement Copyright © 2011 by Amberson Holdings LLC and Stephen Sondheim
Leonard Bernstein Music Publishing Company LLC, Publisher
Boosey & Hawkes, Inc., Sole Agent
Copyright For All Countries   All Rights Reserved

I HAVE A LOVE

TENOR SAX

Copyright © 1957, 1959 by Amberson Holdings LLC and Stephen Sondheim
Copyright Renewed
This arrangement Copyright © 2011 by Amberson Holdings LLC and Stephen Sondheim
Leonard Bernstein Music Publishing Company LLC, Publisher
Boosey & Hawkes, Inc., Sole Agent
Copyright For All Countries   All Rights Reserved

◆5 JET SONG

TENOR SAX

Lyrics by STEPHEN SONDHEIM
Music by LEONARD BERNSTEIN

Copyright © 1957, 1958 by Amberson Holdings LLC and Stephen Sondheim
Copyright Renewed
This arrangement Copyright © 2011 by Amberson Holdings LLC and Stephen Sondheim
Leonard Bernstein Music Publishing Company LLC, Publisher
Boosey & Hawkes, Inc., Sole Agent
Copyright For All Countries   All Rights Reserved

MARIA

TENOR SAX

Lyrics by STEPHEN SONDHEIM
Music by LEONARD BERNSTEIN

Copyright © 1957 by Amberson Holdings LLC and Stephen Sondheim
Copyright Renewed
This arrangement Copyright © 2011 by Amberson Holdings LLC and Stephen Sondheim
Leonard Bernstein Music Publishing Company LLC, Publisher
Boosey & Hawkes, Inc., Sole Agent
Copyright For All Countries   All Rights Reserved

◆ ONE HAND, ONE HEART

TENOR SAX

Lyrics by STEPHEN SONDHEIM
Music by LEONARD BERNSTEIN

Copyright © 1957 by Amberson Holdings LLC and Stephen Sondheim
Copyright Renewed
This arrangement Copyright © 2011 by Amberson Holdings LLC and Stephen Sondheim
Leonard Bernstein Music Publishing Company LLC., Publisher
Boosey & Hawkes, Inc., Sole Agent
Copyright For All Countries   All Rights Reserved

◆⁸ SOMETHING'S COMING

TENOR SAX

Lyrics by STEPHEN SONDHEIM
Music by LEONARD BERNSTEIN

Copyright © 1957 by Amberson Holdings LLC and Stephen Sondheim
Copyright Renewed
This arrangement Copyright © 2011 by Amberson Holdings LLC and Stephen Sondheim
Leonard Bernstein Music Publishing Company LLC., Publisher
Boosey & Hawkes, Inc., Sole Agent
Copyright For All Countries   All Rights Reserved

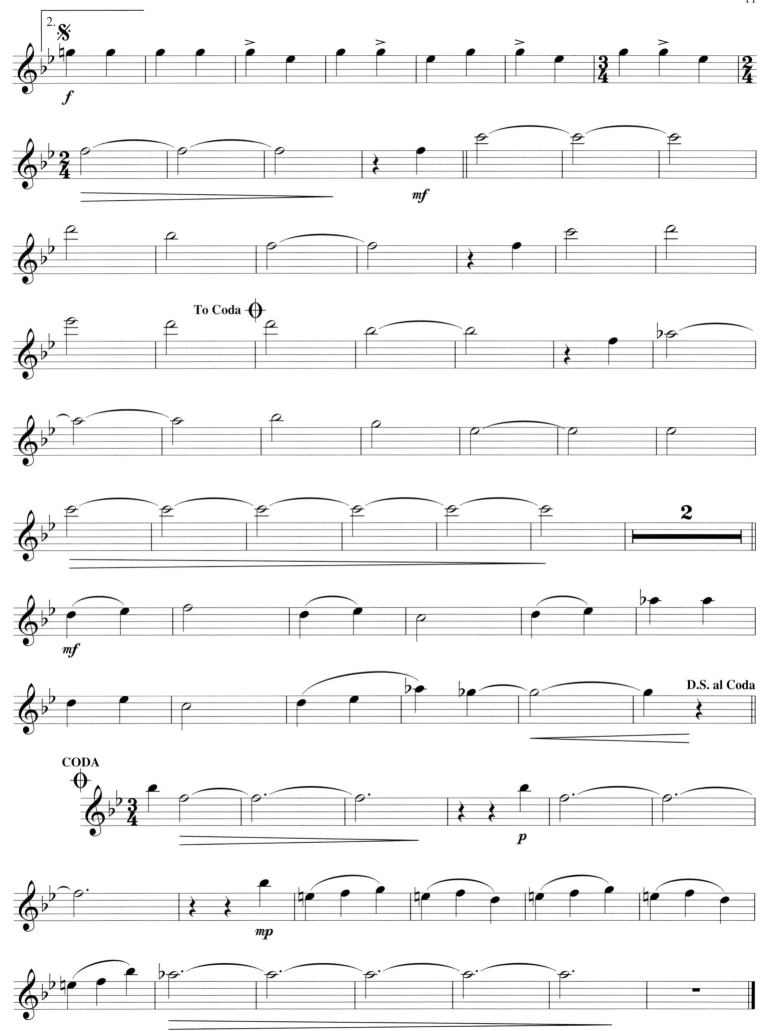

⟐⑨ SOMEWHERE

TENOR SAX

Lyrics by STEPHEN SONDHEIM
Music by LEONARD BERNSTEIN

Copyright © 1957 by Amberson Holdings LLC and Stephen Sondheim
Copyright Renewed
This arrangement Copyright © 2011 by Amberson Holdings LLC and Stephen Sondheim
Leonard Bernstein Music Publishing Company LLC, Publisher
Boosey & Hawkes, Inc., Sole Agent
Copyright for All Countries   All Rights Reserved

⓿ TONIGHT

TENOR SAX

Lyrics by STEPHEN SONDHEIM
Music by LEONARD BERNSTEIN

Copyright © 1957 by Amberson Holdings LLC and Stephen Sondheim
Copyright Renewed
This arrangement Copyright © 2011 by Amberson Holdings LLC and Stephen Sondheim
Leonard Bernstein Music Publishing Company LLC, Publisher
Boosey & Hawkes, Inc., Sole Agent
Copyright for All Countries   All Rights Reserved